Javeria Niazi

Cost of Floods on Pakistan's Economy

Anchor Compact

Niazi, Javeria: Cost of Floods on Pakistan's Economy. Hamburg, Anchor Academic
Publishing 2013
Original title of the thesis: Costs of Floods to Pakistan's Economy

Buch-ISBN: 978-3-95489-066-8
PDF-eBook-ISBN: 978-3-95489-566-3
Druck/Herstellung: Anchor Academic Publishing, Hamburg, 2013
Additionally: Beaconhouse University, Lahore, ,Pakistan, Master Thesis,2010

Bibliografische Information der Deutschen Nationalbibliothek:
Die Deutsche Nationalbibliothek verzeichnet diese Publikation in der Deutschen
Nationalbibliografie; detaillierte bibliografische Daten sind im Internet über
http://dnb.d-nb.de abrufbar

Bibliographical Information of the German National Library:
The German National Library lists this publication in the German National Bibliography.
Detailed bibliographic data can be found at: http://dnb.d-nb.de

All rights reserved. This publication may not be reproduced, stored in a retrieval system
or transmitted, in any form or by any means, electronic, mechanical, photocopying,
recording or otherwise, without the prior permission of the publishers.

Das Werk einschließlich aller seiner Teile ist urheberrechtlich geschützt. Jede Verwertung
außerhalb der Grenzen des Urheberrechtsgesetzes ist ohne Zustimmung des Verlages
unzulässig und strafbar. Dies gilt insbesondere für Vervielfältigungen, Übersetzungen,
Mikroverfilmungen und die Einspeicherung und Bearbeitung in elektronischen Systemen.

Die Wiedergabe von Gebrauchsnamen, Handelsnamen, Warenbezeichnungen usw. in
diesem Werk berechtigt auch ohne besondere Kennzeichnung nicht zu der Annahme,
dass solche Namen im Sinne der Warenzeichen- und Markenschutz-Gesetzgebung als frei
zu betrachten wären und daher von jedermann benutzt werden dürften.

Die Informationen in diesem Werk wurden mit Sorgfalt erarbeitet. Dennoch können
Fehler nicht vollständig ausgeschlossen werden und die Diplomica Verlag GmbH, die
Autoren oder Übersetzer übernehmen keine juristische Verantwortung oder irgendeine
Haftung für evtl. verbliebene fehlerhafte Angaben und deren Folgen.

Alle Rechte vorbehalten

© Anchor Academic Publishing, ein Imprint der Diplomica® Verlag GmbH
http://www.diplom.de, Hamburg 2013
Printed in Germany

Acknowledgements

This thesis could not have been possible without the Will and Grace of Allah Subhanatala. I take this opportunity to express my gratitude towards Dr Hafiz A. Pasha, Dean of School of Social Sciences, my supervisor, under whose guidance and supervision I was able to produce this paper. It was a pleasure and an amazing experience to be taught by him. He has been an encouraging and inspirational teacher. There aren't many people out there who could make a person stand up and want to achieve more in life than there is being offered. I like to also thank the MS Coordinator Muhammad Imran. His help was instrumental and mathematic skills well appreciated. I would especially thank my parents for always standing by me and tolerating my constant mood swings due to lack of sleep and long working hours. Thank you for making it possible for me to be able to produce this thesis.

*DEDICATED
TO MY PARENTS*

Table of Contents

Acknowledgements i
ABSTRACT vi

Chapter 1 1
Chapter 2 9
Chapter 3 13
Chapter 4 25
Chapter 5 31

Appendix 35
REFERENCES 48

List of Tables

Table 1.1 Natural Disasters Comparison 3
Table 1.2 PROVINCE-WISE DAMAGE ASSESSMENT 6
Table 1.3 Sector-wise Damage Assessment 7
Table 3.1 Damage Assessment-NDMA 14
Table 3.2: List of Variables in the Model 18
Table 4.1: Sectoral Growth Rates of GDP in Different Scenarios ....
for 2010-11 and 2011-12 27
Table 4. 2: GDP GROWTH RATES 28

List of Figures

Figure 3.1: Economic Impact of the Flood Shock…………………………………………17

Figure 4.1: Comparison of Growth Rates with Floods and without Floods ………………..28

ABSTRACT

The thesis reviews the available literature on measuring the direct and indirect impacts of natural disasters, both in the short run and in the long run. Based on this review, an attempt is made to quantify the economic impact of the recent floods in Pakistan. This will include not only the estimates emerging from the Damage Needs Assessment by the World Bank and ADB but also derivation of the second round multiplier effects on the GDP by use of the IPP Macroeconomic Model. In addition, an assessment will be made of the prospects for revival of growth.

Keywords: Cost of Floods, Economic impact, Short run and Long run effects, Revival of growth,

CHAPTER ONE

Chapter 1

Introduction

Pakistan is one of the most arid countries in the world with an average annual rainfall of less than 240 mm. It experiences heavy rainfall every year during the monsoon season from July to September. Every year in the summer season the melted ice from the glaciers caused the rivers to flood. However this year the unexpected substantial rainfall during the monsoon period resulted in heavy floods in the absence of adequate infrastructure (dams, barrages, reservoirs). The catastrophe started from the third week of July starting with a heavy rainfall first in the province of Balochistan; then with the second spell of rainfall hitting the province of KPK and trickling down to Punjab and ultimately hitting Sindh. With soaring prices, high level of poverty and the contractionary policy of the IMF program already burdening Pakistan this disaster had come at a time when it was least expected and least desired. The total estimated cost of damages and loss has been estimated to be US$10.06 billion; and the cost of reconstruction ranges from $6.8 billion to $8.9 billion, depending on the level of infrastructure desired.

What does the paper aim to Prove

Though there have been several different researches done on natural disasters around the world focusing on direct cost, this paper will also estimate the indirect effects on the other sectors of the economy; other than agriculture, using a simple structural simultaneous equation model. It is a supply side model and will be useful in defining the cost of different sectors of the economy and to the GDP.

The study consists of five chapters that are set out as follows. The first chapter introduces the topic of the thesis by summarizing how the floods proceeded and affected different regions. In addition it provides facts and figures of the damages and losses incurred in the floods. Chapter two reviews literature on the impact of natural disasters around the world. It summarizes different approaches to find out the economic cost of each disaster and why some countries are affected more than the others. Chapter 3 gives the specification of the model used to derive the effects on different sectors of the economy. Chapter 4 gives results of the simulations of the model. Chapter 5 summarizes the findings and the policy recommendations.

1.1 History of Natural Disasters in Pakistan

1935 Quetta Earthquake

In 1935, the city of Quetta in the province of Baluchistan saw the worst disaster ever seen in the history of Pakistan. 7.7 on the Richter scale the earthquake virtually leveled the city of Quetta. About 60,000 people were killed in one of the deadliest earthquakes of hit South Asia.

1945 Baluchistan earthquake

In 1945 Baluchistan once again faced a devastating earthquake. The earthquake measured 7.8 on the Richter scale with the epicenter about 98 km southwest of the town of Pasni, Balochistan. It not only damaged the property but also led to a 40 foot tsunami causing the death of over 4000 people.

1950 floods

The monsoon rains in 1950 caused a massive flood in Pakistan killing around 2900 people across the country. Even Lahore was not spared from the destruction when the River Ravi flooded and over 100,000 homes were destroyed; leaving around 900,000 people homeless.

1970 East Pakistan

In 1970 East Pakistan saw one of the deadliest tropical cyclone ever recorded. The Bholo Cyclone hit the territory causing up to 500,000 losses of lives primarily as a result of the storm surge that flooded the low-lying islands of Ganges Delta. This disaster is rated to be the worst natural disasters in modern times.

1974 Hunza Earthquake

6.2 on the Richter scale, this earthquake hit Kohistan and surrounding areas including parts of Swat, Hunza and Kashmir in Northern Punjab. About 5300 people were killed; 17000 injured and 97,000 affected.

2000 Drought

The 2000 drought in Baluchistan affected at least 1.2 million people. Over a 100 people died; mostly due to dehydration; according to the official figures. The livestock was greatly affected resulting in large losses. The drought lasted ten months.

2005 Kashmir Quake

In 2005, Kashmir and its surrounding areas were struck by a destructive earthquake measuring 7.6 on the Richter scale. It caused a great deal of damage, resulting in a loss of at least 73,000 live according to the official reports; more than 3.3 million were made homeless. The reconstruction of the infrastructure continues till today.

2007 Cyclone Yemyin

The Cyclone Yemyin hit the coastal areas of Pakistan in early July 2007. At least 730 people died, some 350,000 were displaced and more than 2 million livestock perished.

2010 Hunza Lake Disaster

A landslide in January 2010 in Attabad village in the northern areas of the country; killing 20 people; led to around 40 houses to slide in to the River Hunza. The debris from the landslide caused the river to dam, leading to a formation of a large lake. The lake threatened to flood downstream areas forcing some 20,000 people to leave their homes by June.

1.1 Natural Disasters Comparison

Table 1.1 Comparison of Pakistan's Floods with Major Global Natural Disasters						
	Pakistan flood August 2010	Earthquake Pakistan October 2005	Katrina Cyclone USA	Nargis Cyclone	Tsunami Indian	Haiti Earthquake
Population Affected	20,251,550	3,500,000	500,000	2,420,000	2,273,723	3,200,000
Area Affected (sq. km)	132,000	30,000	N.A	23,500	N.A	13,226
Deaths	1,767	73,338	1,836	84,537	238,000	230,000
Injured	2,865	128,309	N.A	19,359	125,000	300,000
Household Damaged	1,884,708	600,152	200,000	450,000	N.A	250,000

Source: Natural Disaster Management Authority (NDMA), 2nd October, 2010

The floods of 2010 were one of the worst natural disasters ever seen in history. Comparing the floods to the other natural disasters, it can be seen that this disaster caused a record damage to Pakistan. The death rate and the number of people injured may not be high when compared to other natural disasters in the table; but the geographical space and population affected are the largest in these recent floods. The area affected being mostly agricultural land and cropped area; played a devastating role. It not only cut short the food supply, it also affected both the service and manufacturing sectors and took away the source of livelihood of thousands of people. The population affected by the floods is so huge in both scale and destruction that it is more than all the above natural disasters put together.

1.3 How it all Began

Beginning of the monsoon season is the most looked forward time as it brings the much needed rain to the arid region of Pakistan. But in 2010 we saw the highest recorded rainfall in a decade; submerging vast areas and causing people to evacuate these areas. The heavy rainfall began and continued for days in the regions of Balochistan followed closely by a second spell of heavy monsoon rains over Khyber Pakhtunkhwa, which commenced in the last week of July 2010 and persisted up till first few days of August. Khyber-Pakhtunkhwa (KPK); flooding the cities of Peshawar, Nowshera, Swat, Charsada, etc. and cutting off these areas from the rest of the province and closing all routes towards the flood affected areas.

These rains generated unmatched flood flows in the major as well as secondary and tertiary rivers, including the nullahs in KPK, Punjab and then Sindh. The local rivers and nullahs in Baluchistan also saw extraordinary floods. The river Indus, at some of the control points in Punjab and Sindh, along with River Swat, Panjkora and Kabul experienced historic flood flows.

The heavy rainfall caused the river banks to burst, flooding the low regions and those nearer to the banks. Many houses, schools, roads were either severely damaged or destroyed leaving the people without food, shelter and medical attention. With half the province of KPK under water barely surviving the blow from the natural disaster, the rainfall then hit Punjab and affected the Indus River Basin.

The flow of the water from the heavy rainfall and the rivers pushed its way from KPK to Punjab as it made its way downstream to southern Punjab and Sindh. Though the Metrological (MET) Department and Natural Disaster Management Authority (NDMA) of Pakistan had forewarned the people to spare them from the demolition; the floods still managed to cause major damages to the people, land, infrastructure, etc.

Houses, schools, hospitals, electricity poles, transformers, cropped areas, standing crops, cattle, sheeps, animals; nothing was spared by the wrath of the flood water. Though millions of people lost their homes, shelter, and their income earning assets; the death toll wasn't as high as compared to the other natural disasters seen in Pakistan.

People moved to safer areas in the hope of being spared from the destruction. But even reaching the safe areas the people were affected in one way or the other. The authorities were a slow in relief efforts for the flood victims. There were food and water shortages, and shelter wasn't available to most of the victims. The people were in need of proper medical facilities. The army played a major role in trying to help the people reach safe grounds and support those who managed to get there on their own.

The private sector, civilians and a number of both national and international organizations have all put in every effort to generate funds for these people. Food items, clothing, shelter, etc. were collected in large quantity and taken to the flood affected areas. Till present day, relief efforts are still taking place. The government along with international agencies like the UN, World Bank and Asian Development Bank are working towards restoration of the affected areas. Estimate of the damage and costs of reconstruction have already been made and mentioned later in the study.

1.4 Damage Assessment Analysis

A total of 78 districts were hit, 2,092,600 hectares of cropped area was destroyed, 20,184,550 population was affected, 1,985 people died, 2,926 people were injured and 1,744,471 houses were damaged; according to the official report of the Natural Disaster Management Authority (NDMA) on 14th November.

The figures of the damage and reconstruction costs released on the 14th of November by the World Bank and ADB at the inauguration of the Pakistan Development Forum are listed in the table below. Most of the figures coincide with those presented by the officials in Pakistan with a few discrepancies here and there.

Table 1.2 PROVINCE-WISE DAMAGE ASSESSMENT

Province	Damages/Losses Million $	Reconstruction Costs Million $
Sindh	4400	3100
Punjab	2600	1300
KPK	1200	2200
Balochistan	620	684

Source: Pakistan Development Forum, Express Tribune, 15th November

Table 1.2 and 1.3 show the cost of the losses incurred due to floods and the reconstruction costs on both the provincial and sectoral level. The total cost of the losses and damage is taken out to be around $10,056 million and the total cost of reconstruction ranges from $6799 million to $8900 million depending upon the level of reconstruction. If the same infrastructure is built then the cost incurred will be $6800 million. If a better infrastructure is constructed then the cost will be $7418 million. For even higher standards of infrastructure the cost incurred will be $8915 million.

Table 1.3 SECTOR-WISE DAMAGE ASSESSMENT

Sectors	Damages/ Losses	Needs: Option 1	Option 2	Option 3
	million $	million $		
Irrigation	278	427	427	982
Housing	1,588	1,483	1,690	2,206
Agriculture	5.045	257	670	1,049
Transport and Communication	1,328	2,356	2,356	2,356
Energy	309	106	106	106
Livelihood Support		683	683	683
Private Sector	282	102	102	129
Education	311	505	505	505
Health	50	49	49	49
Water and Sanitation	109	74	74	94
Governance	70	58	58	58
Financial	674	463	463	463
Environment	12	209	209	209
DRM		27	27	27
Total	10,056	6,799	7,418	8,915

Source: Pakistan development Forum

CHAPTER TWO

Chapter 2

Literature Review

Hallegatte S. and Ghil M. (2008) with an endogenous business cycle model study the macroeconomic response towards natural disaster in which a recurring behavior takes place due to the flux of the investment-profit. The model concludes a greater response towards natural disasters during expansions than during recession because the exogenous shock amplifies the pre-existing disequilibria. In recessions, however, the existence of unused resources triggers the damping of stock. Higher output variability is also seen in response to the stochastic productivity shocks during expansions as compared to in recessions.

Long F. (1978) assembles the data available on consequences of natural disaster on Third World agriculture. These consequences provide an explanation of the lack of self capability of the low income countries; it also explains the occurrence of hunger and increasing poverty. He prefers a systemized data collection that can be used to study the effects of natural disasters. A proper mechanism can be planned through that data to protect agriculture in disaster prone countries. With a planning system the adverse effects of natural disasters can be mitigated.

Toya H. and Skidmore M. (2005) analyze the data of natural disasters impact over a period of time to study the extent to which the human and economic losses from natural disasters are reduced as economies develop. They undertake two sets of regressions for determining the relationship between the level of development and disaster impacts. One set of regressions analyze the impact of natural disasters on income whereas the second set of regressions focuses on economic damages. They establish that countries with higher income, higher educational attainment, and greater openness, more complete financial systems and smaller governments experience fewer losses.

Rodriguez-Oreggia E., Fuente A. and Torre R. (2008) examine the effects of natural disaster on social indicators such as HDI and different poverty levels at the municipal level in Mexico. To find the effects the analysis controls for a set of geographical and natural characteristics of location. Also control is set for precondition institutional, economic and demographic characteristics for heterogeneity. The paper uses an adjusted difference-in-difference regression on data for 2000 and 2005. The results demonstrate a significant fall in social indicators from natural disaster and especially floods and droughts, including HDI and the level of poverty. There is a major impact from natural disasters on reducing the HDI and also increasing poverty.

Bergholt D. and Lujala P. (2010) relied on econometric methods for the investigation of economic consequences of natural disasters and their linkage to armed civil conflict for the period 1980-2007; panel data and OLS regressions are used as the methodology. Geographical and hydro-meteorological disasters have a negative impact on income growth. But there is no significant evidence that supports the argument that negative effects of disasters increases the likelihood of armed civil conflicts.

Popp A. (2006) explores the relationship between natural disasters and long term economic growth. Several key macro-economic variables, most notably technology that can increase or decrease economic growth is affected by natural disasters. After the disaster recovery is very important and the institutions of the country determine how the economy makes progress.

Rasunussen N.T. (2004) provides an assessment of cross country natural disasters occurrence. The countries are compared along four dimensions: the number of events divided by land area; the number of events divided by population; the number of affected persons divided by total population and damages divided by GDP. The analysis demonstrates that the most disaster prone areas in the world are the small island states especially countries of Eastern Caribbean. Natural disasters are found to have a discernable macro-economic impact, including large affects on fiscal and external balances, pointing to an important role of stabilization measures.

Pelling M., Ozerdem A. and Barakot S. (2002) throw light on the impact of natural disasters on developing nations. The analysis also shows the types of losses the country faces and the effect on long run growth. In the paper three types of losses are mentioned; direct losses, indirect losses and secondary losses. The respective results depict that economic growth declines and the debt burden increases as a result of disasters. The post disaster period in the short run offers opportunities for acquiring foreign capital, remittances, foreign aid, and reinsurance payment;

but it is only a short term solution and is insufficient to compensate for all the losses especially those due to systemic and secondary effects.

Vakis R. (2006) asserts that natural disasters have a huge impact on social and economic welfare. Policies to manage them need to be integrated and well grounded to the specifications of natural hazards as well as local capacities in terms of fiscal, administrative and economic capabilities. A well designed natural disaster management strategy crucially depends on carefully assessing and planning responses before, during and after the disaster occurs. This policy note discusses the complementary role that Social Protection can play in the formation of an effective strategy for natural disasters management.

Benson C. and Clay J. E. (2004) examine the short-term and long term economic and financial impacts of natural disasters, relying mostly on in-depth case studies of overall sensitivity to natural hazards in the small island economy of Dominica; public finance consequences of disasters in Bangladesh; and the economic consequences of climate variability in Malawi and Southern Africa. Policy implications are drawn, and, where appropriate, recommendations are made. Finally, directions for future research and cooperation are outlined.

CHAPTER THREE

Chapter 3

THEORETICAL FRAMEWORK AND EMPIRICAL RESULTS

Given that the current floods in Pakistan have had an impact on all the sectors of the economy. Handling these problems would require a model that could simultaneously capture the major relations among different sectors of the economy and thereby trace through the indirect and secondary effects on the economy.

The purpose of this chapter is to develop a formal economic framework. The model will be used to quantify the cost of floods to the Pakistan's economy in terms of lost output. The model is particularly developed keeping in view the present economic scenario of the country and will be used to forecast short to medium run economic outlook of the country in the aftermath of the floods.

3.1 Structure of the Model

The model contains 4 equations: 2 behavioral equations and 2 identities. Including the exogenous variables, there are a total of 10 variables in the model database. These are enough to give a richer account of interaction between the three major sectors of the economy; the agriculture sector, manufacturing sector, and the services sector. Thus, through the model, what we are trying to see the impact of the flood on the GDP of the Pakistan.

3.2 Direct Impacts

Agriculture sector was most directly hit by the floods, which only damaged the standing crops but also damaged the agricultural infrastructure like irrigation channels and watercourses, farm to market roads, and the power distribution network in the rural areas. The water also drowned many livestock along with fodder storage facilities which resulted in shortages. This happened in all the four provinces. It is estimated that almost 2.245 million hectares of cropped area was affected. The livestock lost is around 1.4 million with 14 million at risk due to fodder shortages.

According to the PDMA of Punjab, 461 irrigation channels were damaged and 2899 kilometer of roads was affected badly by the floods. A summary of the damages has been given in the table 3.1.

Table 3.1 DAMAGE ASSESSMENT

Province	Area affected (Sq. km)	Deaths	Injured	Houses damaged	Total affected districts	Population affected	Crop area (hectares)	Cattle head
Balochistan	322	48	98	75,261	12	700,000	255,237	55,501
KPK	Awaiting	1,156	1,198	200,799	24	3,800,000	205,347	52,757
Punjab	14,047	110	350	509,814	11	8,200,000	774,610	3,572
Sind	30,132	393	1,202	1,114,629	17	7,184,550	1,056,758	263,703
AJK	30,132	393	1,202	1,114,629	17	7,184,550	1,056,758	263,703
G-B	7,500	183	60	2,830	7	100,000	3,635	4,669
Grand Total		1961	2,995	1,910,439	78	20,184,550	2,326,407	324,982

Source: NDMA   (As of 2nd Oct, 2010)

Therefore, the most direct impact was on agriculture both crops and livestock. The medium term and long term affects are the indirect affects due to the damage of infrastructure which will limit the production capacity of the agricultural economy. Till the time the infrastructure is rebuilt, production losses will continue. According to the Provincial Governments the recovery could take two to three years.

Damage to shelter also affects the GDP. This is due to the loss in the rental values of property damaged by the floods. There are no precise calculations made by the National Income Accounts of Pakistan to capture the yearly fluctuations in the Ownership of Dwelling sector. Therefore, it is unlikely that this loss will be allowed for by FBS when the GDP for 2010-11 is estimated. It is also possible that rural small-scale and cottage industry has been affected by the floods here also the FBS is unable to accurately measure the value added of the in small-scale manufacturing, on an annual basis.

3.3 Indirect Impacts

We turn to the linkages of the agricultural sector with the rest of the economy. Understanding these relationships is necessary when the indirect effects of the floods on the economy are to be quantified. These linkages are identified below.

3.3.1 Agriculture to Manufacturing

Around 40% of the manufacturing sector of Pakistan is agro-based industry, both in terms of processing agriculture inputs and in providing inputs like fertilizer for agricultural production. Textiles, sugar, leather, and cigarettes are the major industries of Pakistan which rely on raw materials like cotton, sugarcane, hides and skins and tobacco. Production of all these inputs has been severely affected by the floods. Already, cotton (phutti) arrivals have slowed down and stand short by about 15 percent in relation to the level last year. Though a large quantity of cotton is going to be imported, the production of yarn and value added textiles will be adversely affected. The sugarcane crop is likely to have faced a damage of 15 to 20 percent. The sugar factories will face high prices for what is left of the sugarcane and achieve production levels which are significantly lower than last year.

To top it off, as the planting season starts for the Rabi crops, the demand for fertilizers is likely to be reduced if the land for cultivation is still under water or if the fertilizer and seeds packages being provided by the provincial governments do not reach the farmers. There may also be a delay in the return of the displaced population due to the slow progress of rehabilitation work in some areas.

The industries which have been impacted by the loss in agricultural production have a total weight of 50.63% in the Index of Industrial Production. Already the month of August 2010, there was a decline of 3 percent in the large scale manufacturing sector in relation to the level in the corresponding month of the previous year. Most of the agro-based industries have shown a negative growth and this will become more pronounced in the coming months.

A relatively less obvious impact is likely to be due to the lack of growth in the rural purchasing power due to lower marketed surplus of agricultural produce. With the phenomenal increase in wheat procurement price by the government in the year 2008-09, for example, rural incomes increased rapidly. This resulted in an increase in the demand of durable goods like tractors, cars, motorcycles, TVs, fans, freezers, etc. but in the year 2010-11 this is not likely to happen given the loss of production due to floods. Growth of industries catering to the rural market will probably be relatively low this year.

3.3.2 Agriculture to Services:

Agriculture is the primary sector and services the tertiary sector of the economy. There is, like with the manufacturing sector, a two way relationship between these sectors. The loss in the agriculture production due to the floods will have an adverse affect on a number of services as listed below.

- Wholesale and retail trade

    According to the estimates of FBS trading margins on agricultural production in the wholesale and retail trade sector makes up about 75% of the value added. This includes commodities like milk, wheat, rice, cotton, vegetables, fruits and various manufactured goods. The growth in this sector, especially with the shortage of cotton, is probably going to be negatively affected in 2010-11 due to the floods.

- Transport and Communication

    Direct affect of the floods on the infrastructure has already been explained. Other than that, the fall in the production levels of both the agriculture and manufacturing goods will imply less demand for transportation. Road traffic volumes, which contribute around 70 percent of the value added of the sector will be badly affected.

- Banking and insurance

    Outstanding loans of farmers by the commercial banks and the specialized agricultural development bank are approximately Rs 200 billion. Some of these loans are at risk of turning into a bad debt because many farmers are not be in a position to pay back their loans after losing their assets and incomes due to the floods. The resulting decline in the profitability will reduce the value addition in the banking and insurance sector in 2010-11. The direct and indirect sectoral impacts of the floods are gives in figure 1.

Figure 3.1: Economic Impact of the Flood Shock

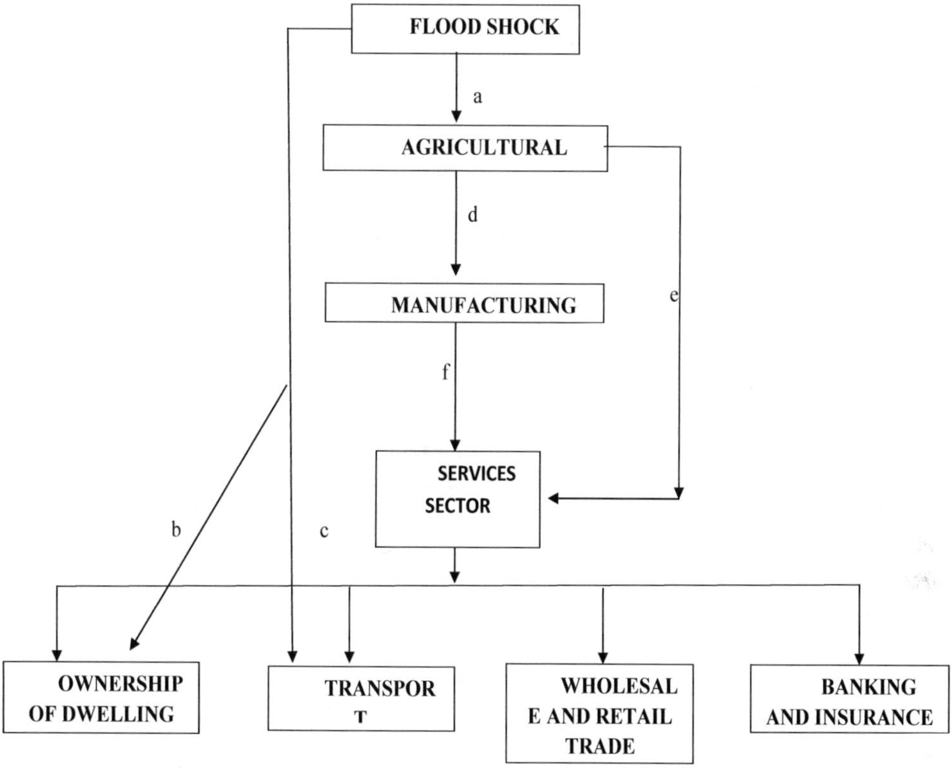

```
                    FLOOD SHOCK
                         |
                         a
                         ↓
                    AGRICULTURAL ─────┐
                         |            |
                         d            |
                         ↓            e
                    MANUFACTURING     |
                         |            |
                         f            |
                         ↓            |
                    SERVICES ←────────┘
                    SECTOR
        b        c      |
   ┌────┬────────┬──────┼──────────┬──────────┐
   ↓    ↓        ↓                 ↓          ↓
OWNERSHIP   TRANSPORT        WHOLESALE     BANKING
OF DWELLING                  AND RETAIL    AND INSURANCE
                             TRADE
```

Direct impact = a, b, c

Indirect impact = d, e, f

3.4 Data Sources and Description

The data taken for this research is collected from the two standard sources of data in Pakistan. These include various issues of Economic Survey of Pakistan and Annual Report of the State Bank of Pakistan. The time period of the data is from 1980-81 to 2009-10. Note that all the variables taken are the growth rates and except for the real interest rate. In the table below each of the variable is described in detail.

Table 3.2: List of Variables in the Model

Name of Variable	Symbol	Definition
Agriculture Sector Growth Rate	GA	It is the growth rate of the value added of the agriculture sector to the GDP at constant prices of 1999-2000.
Manufacturing Sector Growth Rate	GM	It is the growth rate of the value added of the manufacturing sector to the GDP at constant prices of 1999-2000.
Services Sector Growth Rate	GS	It is the growth rate of the value added of the services sector to the GDP at constant prices of 1999-2000.
GDP Growth Rate	GY	It is the growth rate of the GDP at constant prices of 1999-2000.
Real Rate of Interest	R	The real interest rate is taken as the difference between the nominal interest rate (measured as the weighted average rate of return of advances) and the inflation rate.
Growth Rate of Exports	GX	The growth rate of exports of goods and services.
Growth Rate of Home Remittances	GHR	The growth rate of home remittances accruing to the Pakistani economy.
Share of Agricultural Sector in the GDP	S_A	The share of the agricultural sector to the GDP of Pakistan.
Share of Manufacturing Sector in the GDP	S_M	The share of the manufacturing sector to the GDP of Pakistan.
Share of Services Sector in the GDP	S_S	The share of the services sector to the GDP of Pakistan.

3.4.1 Agricultural Sector

In the model, the agricultural sector is taken exogenously by the identity.

$$GA = \overline{GA} \quad \ldots \ldots \ldots \ldots (1)$$

The growth in agricultural sector is taken as an exogenous variable because its growth rate is dependent upon a number of factors which cannot be predicted with certainty and that cannot be controlled. These factors make the growth rate of the agricultural sector uncertain too. The factors include weather conditions in the country, floods, and other natural calamities.

3.4.2 Manufacturing Sector

The growth rate in the manufacturing sector is behavioral determine by the equation:

$$GM = \beta_0 + \beta_1 GA + \beta_2 GY + \beta_3 R + \beta_4 GX \quad \ldots \ldots \ldots \ldots (2)$$

$$\text{while } \beta_1, \beta_2, \beta_4 > 0 \text{ and } \beta_3 < 0$$

As it can be seen from the equation, the growth rate in manufacturing sector, *GM*, is dependent upon the growth rate in the agricultural sector, *GA*, the overall growth rate of the economy, *GY*, the real rate of interest rate, *R*, and the growth rate in the exports of goods and services, *GX*. The agricultural sector is included as an independent variable because it provides raw materials to almost 40% of main agro-based industries in the manufacturing sector. Thus, the growth rate in the agriculture sector directly affects the growth rate in the manufacturing sector.

Other three variables in the equation measure the response on the demand. That is, if the GDP grows at a faster rate, it will increase the income of the people which will in turn increase the demand. More demand means, there will be more production taking place in the economy. Thus, when the *GY* is increases/decreases the growth in the manufacturing sector also increases/decreases.

Similarly, the faster the increase in the growth rate of exports, *GX*, the higher the growth rate of the manufacturing sector will be. Growth in export means that there is a high demand for the domestic goods in the international market, so there will an increase in the growth rate of the manufacturing sector. By trading externally the producers get an entrance in the foreign market, explore new avenues and sell their product at a higher price than in the domestic market.

The last variable in the equation is the real interest rate, R. It is a policy variable and has a negative impact on the manufacturing sector, from the investment side. As the rate of interest increases it makes costly for the producers to invest in expanding production capacity and ultimately reduces the growth of the manufacturing sector.

3.4.3 Services Sector

The services sector is the largest sector of the economy. It contributes around 55 percent to the GDP and is related directly and indirectly to both the manufacturing sector and the agricultural sector. In the model, it is behaviorally determined by the equation:

$$GS = \sigma_0 + \sigma_1[GA + GM] + \sigma_2 GY + \sigma_3 GHR \dots \dots \dots (3)$$

$$\text{While } \sigma_1, \sigma_2, \sigma_3 > 0$$

The growth rate in the services sector is dependent upon the sum of the growth rate in the agriculture sector and the growth rate in the manufacturing sector $[GA + GM]$ and growth rate of the home remittances (GHR). When there is growth in the agriculture and manufacturing sector, there will be a need for certain services like transport, storage and communication; wholesale and retail trade; finance and insurance. Similarly, the growth in the GDP and home remittances will lead to an increase in the above mentioned services. The increase in the home remittances will lead to an increase in the banking and insurance sectors. Other variables which could impact on the growth of the services include the growth of the public expenditures, imports, etc.

3.4.4 Gross Domestic Product

The gross domestic product (GDP) is the sum of the value addition of all the sectors of the economy; it is, therefore, given by the following identity:

$$GY = S_A \cdot GA + S_M \cdot GM + (1 - S_A - S_M) \cdot GS \dots \dots \dots (4)$$

where,

$$S_S = (1 - S_A - S_M)$$

It can be seen from the above identity, that the growth rate of the gross domestic product, GY, is the weighted sum of growth rates of the three main sector of the economy; agriculture, manufacturing, and services sector. The weights are measured as their percentage contribution to the overall economy of the Pakistan.

3.5 Linkages in the Model

The equations in the model are interlinked. The growth in the agriculture sector has an impact on the growth of the manufacturing and services sectors. Manufacturing sector in turn has an impact on the services sector. Similarly, the growth in the GDP has an impact especially on demand in the manufacturing sector.

3.5.1 List of Endogenous and Exogenous Variables in the Model

The following are the endogenous and exogenous variables in the model:

3.5.1.2 Endogenous Variables

- Growth rate of manufacturing sector (GM)
- Growth rate of services sector (GS)
- Growth rate of gross domestic product (GY)

3.5.1.3 Exogenous Variables

- Growth rate of agriculture sector (GA)
- Growth rate of exports of goods and services (GX)
- Growth rate of home remittances (GHR)
- Real rate of interest (R)
- Share of agricultural sector in the GDP (S_A)
- Share of manufacturing sector in the GDP (S_M)
- Share of services sector in the GDP (S_S)

As mentioned earlier, other exogenous variables were included in the model as follows:

- Growth Rate of foreign aid
- Growth Rate of Public Investment
- Growth Rate of Public Expenditure
- Growth Rate of Tax Burden in Manufacturing

But they were excluded from the analysis due to the relatively low levels of significance.

3.6 Empirical Results

This section presents the empirical results of the estimated model. Compared to the theoretical model explained in the last section, the estimated model equations show some changes. These include, *inter alia,* the specification of the simpler lag structures of the dependent variable. In all the equations below, the t-statistic of each coefficient is reported in the parentheses below the value of the coefficient. The DW-stat is the Durbin-Watson test statistic of serial correlation and F-ratio is the F-statistic is right below the value of the t-statistic. In each equation, the variables are in growth terms, except for the real interest rate variable in the manufacturing sector equation. The asterisks *, **, and *** in the equations denote that the coefficients are significant at the level of 1, 5, and 10 percent.

3.6.1 Behavioural Equations

3.6.1.1 The Manufacturing Sector

$$GM = 1.1008 + 1.2433GY + 0.0519GX - 0.2720R$$
$$(0.837) \quad (5.89)^* \quad (1.138) \quad (-1.817)^{***}$$

Adjusted-R^2 = 0.7397, DW-Stat = 2.156

F-ratio = 17.486

(0.000)

3.6.1.2 The Services Sector

$$GS = 1.2071 + 0.1424[GA + GM] + 0.0131 GHR + 0.5283 GS_{-1}$$
$$(1.818)^{***} \ (3.99)^* \qquad (1.159) \qquad (4.927)^*$$

Adjusted-R^2 = 0.6955,   DW-Stat = 1.998

F-ratio = 16.992

(0.000)

Identities

The Agriculture Sector

$$GA = \overline{GA}$$

The Gross Domestic Product

$$GY = SA \cdot GA + SM \cdot GM + (1 - SA - SM) \cdot GS$$

CHAPTER FOUR

Chapter 4

SIMULATIONS OF THE MODEL

The model explained in the previous chapter is subjected to a number of simulations. The simulations are run on E-views. To run the simulations, we have taken certain values of the three exogenous variables used in the model; GA, GX and GHR. The growth rates for agriculture are taken keeping in mind two case scenarios; loss due to the floods in the fiscal year 2010-11 and the recovery from the floods in the fiscal year 2011-12. The magnitude of loss taken in the agriculture sector in terms of growth ranges from of 0 to -5%; depicting both the worst and best case scenarios. For 2011-12, the level of recovery is taken in the range of growth of 1% to 4%; which gives us the least and most favourable rate of recovery. The predicted values for both GX and GHR are on the basis of current trends. These simulations give us a range of all the possible outcomes with regards to the growth rate of the economy in 2011 and 2012.

4.1 Magnitude if Exogenous Variables

The exogenous variables as mentioned before are growth rate of agriculture (GA), growth rate of net exports (GX), real interest rate (R) and growth rate of home-remittances (GHR).

4.1.1 Agriculture

This sector was the worst hit in these recent floods. The impact on the growth rate of agriculture is estimated as follows:

Total Cropped Area affected = 2.092 million hectares
Total Cropped Area = 23.80 million hectares
Share of area affected: 2.092/23.80 = 0.9 = 9%
Expected Growth Rate was 3.8% in 2010-11 in the absence of floods.
Therefore, net impact = 5%
As such, we have assumed the maximum fall in the value added in the agricultural sector 2010-11 is 5%.

4.1.2 Net Exports

The growth of exports is taken for the last three months from July to September of 8.2%. We assume that this growth rate remains the same for the whole year, 2010-11 and for 2011-12 at 6.8%, which is close to the long-term trend growth rate of exports.

4.1.3 Home- Remittances

The values taken for remittances are 19.0% for the year 2010-11 and 21% for the year 2011-12, in line with the recent buoyancy in these flows.

Also the reason behind the highest expected increase in home remittances is that the Pakistani residents living abroad will now be sending more relief funds in to the country. Organizations and communities around the world are helping Pakistan with the relief efforts and this too is bringing more money in the economy in terms of foreign exchange. All those Pakistani who have stake in the country will be sending back monetary aid to their families and friends.

4.1.4 Real Interest rate

This is assumed at 3.5 percentage points in 2010-11 and 2011-12.

4.2 Results of Simulation of Model

Altogether, 48 simulations are undertaken of the model, results of which are given in the Statistical Appendix. In our judgment the range of outcomes is given in the tables below.

Table 4.1: Sectoral Growth Rates of GDP in Different Scenarios for 2010-11 and 2011-12

	Likely Growth Rate	Projected Growth Rates		
Most favourable Scenario	GA	GM	GS	GDP
2010-11	0	4.8	3.8	3.3
2011-12	4	7.5	5.1	5.5
Likely Scenario				
2010-11	-3	3.1	3.1	1.9
2011-12	3	6.4	4.5	4.7
Most unfavourable Scenario				
2010-11	-5	1.9	2.7	1
2011-12	2	5.6	4	4

Therefore, the growth rate of GDP in 2010-11 is likely to range between 1 and 3.3 percent, with the most likely scenario at just below 2 percent. Depending upon the pace of reconstruction work the GDP growth rate in 2011-12 could lie between 4 to 5.5 percent, with the likely outcome at 4.7 percent.

Given the most likely scenario the cumulative direct and indirect cost of the floods in terms of lost GDP is Rs 445 billion by 2011-12 at 2009-10 prices. This is based on the assumption that in the absence of the floods, the GDP would have increased by 4.5% in 2010-11 and 5.0% in 2011-12. In dollar terms, the loss over the next two years in the level of GDP is just over $5 billion.

Table 4. 2: GDP GROWTH RATES

	GDP growth rate	
Year	without floods	with floods
2009-10	4.1	4.1
2010-11	4.5	1.9
2011-12	5.0	4.7

Figure 4.1: Comparison of Growth Rates with Floods and without Floods

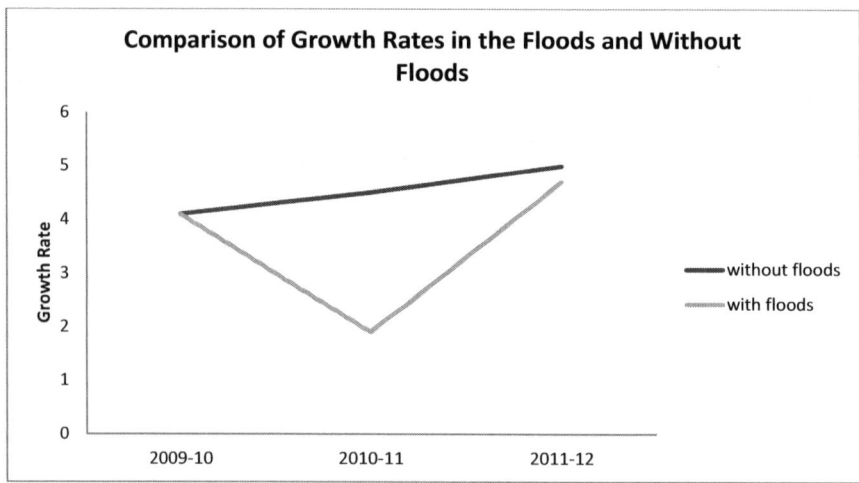

Figure 1: Trends in GDP growth rates

4.2.1 Sensitivity Analysis

The model indicates that the direct and indirect of effects of a fall in agricultural production in 2010-11 are, more or less, equal in magnitude. A 1% fall in the growth rate of agriculture has the direct impact of reducing the growth rate of the GDP by about 0.22 percentage points while the indirect effects, due to the negative impact on the manufacturing sector and service sector, is about 0.25 percentage points.

CHAPTER FIVE

Chapter 5

CONCLUSION

With the world climate changing, human beings are faced with natural disasters ever so often. These climatic changes are resulting in fierce storms, tornadoes, hurricane, cyclones, floods and drought. The floods 2010 have been the most devastating natural disaster to ever hit Pakistan. Even the 2005 earthquake couldn't match the destruction it caused. Though the death toll wasn't as high as the other disasters, its affect is the greatest

The paper starts by summarizing step by step how the floods impacted different regions. It proceeded further with the history of floods in Pakistan and its comparison with major natural disasters around the world. It states the latest figures of the damage and reconstruction costs that Pakistan will be incurring due to the floods.

The point of working on this topic isn't to just repeat what has already been told several times in the past few months. It is to show exactly how much the economy is going to be losing. The overall loss has already been given but there hasn't been any work done explaining the affects of one sector on the other sectors of the economy; impact of agriculture loss on manufacturing and services sectors.

The paper takes the data from the Economic Survey (various issues) and the State Bank of Pakistan's annual report (various issues) from the period of 1980-81 to 2009-10. To find out to the linkage between different sectors and their impact on one another, a growth model has been designed. The model shows the supply side effects on the whole economy. The losses incurred are in terms of decrease in the output. As the agricultural sector has direct links with both the manufacturing and services sector the loss in agricultural production will be shown on both these sectors.

Manufacturing will be affected more than the services sector as forty percent of the industries are agro based. There'll be impact on the services as well but it will be of a lesser magnitude than that on the industries. Hence the national income will face a low growth rate compared to the predicted value due to the affects of negative to low growth rates in all three sectors of the economy.

Different growth rates in agriculture for the next two years (2010-11 and 2011-12) ranging from -5 to -1 for the first year (2010-11) have been taken to show the affects of the floods; and 1 to 4 for the year after that (2011-12) which portrays the level of recovery from the disaster. Two different values of the growth rate in exports and home remittances are also taken to be used with the values of the growth in agriculture. With these values simulations are projected which give us a vivid picture of the economy with different growth rates.

From the simulation three different scenarios are taken which explain the most likely situation, the least likely situation and the most favourable situation that the economy will probably be facing. The results from the model and damage assessment report clearly tell us what Pakistan will be facing in terms of production loss and recovery. The results are estimates that we have assessed on the basis of past data and current situation in the country.

The adverse affects of natural disasters are mostly felt in third world countries and those which have a small land area and high population density. Developing countries like Pakistan do not have proper infrastructure facilities available to them; the income national isn't high enough to reimburse the affected population; do not have proper facilities to act upon when such situations arise; and they are not trained in the matters of evacuation. Due to these factors the whole isn't isolated from the affects of the disaster. With small land area and high population density the natural disaster affects are very high. There are fewer places to be used as shelter or safe ground. More people in the area the more they are affected. In case of Pakistan all these factors were present which contributed towards

We conclude the paper by giving policy recommendations which aim to prepare the country from any future natural disaster. Natural disaster can be foreseen but they cannot be stopped. The policy makers should work towards in protecting people and national assets from the worst affects of such disasters.

Policy Recommendations

The literature reviewed on natural disasters for this paper gives us a vivid picture of why some countries are more severely damaged by natural disasters and some don't. Reason behind this is that natural disasters are beyond human control. One cannot stop a natural disaster from occurring. All one can do is take precautionary measures to avoid the worst of its damage from taking place.

Pakistan is a natural disaster prone country. Every year the summer season floods the rivers which cause damage to the areas near the river banks. Other than that Pakistan has faced it share of earthquakes, cyclones and floods over the past years. It is time for the government organizations to act upon taking proper precautionary measures to lessen the destruction from any future natural disaster.

The policies that I recommend after working on this thesis are as follows:

- There is a need to enhance early warning systems. This can be done by restoring and enhancing the performance of key elements of the country's natural disaster early warning system and develop a multi hazard integrated decision support and alert system.
- The government should increase community preparedness and awareness through promotion of community based disaster risk management and education.
- There should be an early initiation and completion of national multi-hazard risk mapping to define the national hazard risk environment and also develop a strategy for catastrophe risk financing.
- For Disaster Risk Management (DRM) there has to be a management study of NDMA and existing parallel DRM structures for assimilations.
- There should be development and integration of DRM in education and awareness building at all levels.
- By starting Learning-Teaching process the government can restore confidence of the people in the abilities of the government.
- Partially damaged schools should be a priority to the fully damaged ones.

- Basic services of the energy sector should be restored followed by rehabilitation of supporting infrastructure and restore projects which were completely damaged by the floods.
- Immediate issues relating to environment should be addressed like contaminated drinking water, disease vectors, hazardous waste, safe waste disposal and debris disposal.
- The authorities as well as the privet sector should initiate additional studies for existing data gaps on environment issues like landslide, stagnant water, campsite restoration, hazardous spills and cultural heritage.
- Fresh credit should be extended to the affected areas for the revival of business activities especially for agriculture and medium and small scale industries.
- Government needs to ensure adequate and timely fund flow. It should establish a proper accountability system with transparent flows of funds.
- Inter government communication needs to be improved. Vertical, federal to district, and horizontal, of one department with another, coordination should be clarified.
- Measures should be taken to improve disaster preparedness and response of the health sector.
- Staff at district and tehsil levels should be trained to respond to emergencies and take lead in coordination with NDMA and PDMA.
- For the irrigation infrastructure damage, reconstruction with remodeling should be done with the view of building safer structures.
- Census should be conducted to identify different social groups and target support for vulnerable groups.
- Each province has different dynamics. Pre-existing social-economic differences, social relations, geography, and governance structures require a customized approach. Local government should be strengthened to deliver services, get communities and CSOs to work with them.

Appendix

Chapter 4

Equation 1

Dependent Variable: GS
Method: Least Squares
Date: 11/11/10   Time: 15:42
Sample (adjusted): 1982 2010
Included observations: 29 after adjustments

Variable	Coefficient	Std. Error	t-Statistic	Prob.
C	1.207123	0.663932	1.818142	0.0815
GA+GM	0.142407	0.035691	3.990020	0.0005
GHR	0.013071	0.011282	1.158583	0.2580
GS(-1)	0.528294	0.107452	4.916570	0.0001
D1	-2.785019	0.753846	-3.694414	0.0011

R-squared	0.739042	Mean dependent var		5.479310
Adjusted R-squared	0.695549	S.D. dependent var		1.781528
S.E. of regression	0.982995	Akaike info criterion		2.959160
Sum squared resid	23.19071	Schwarz criterion		3.194901
Log likelihood	-37.90783	Hannan-Quinn criter.		3.032991
F-statistic	16.99221	Durbin-Watson stat		1.997543
Prob(F-statistic)	0.000001			

Equation 2

Dependent Variable: GM
Method: Least Squares
Date: 11/11/10   Time: 15:47
Sample: 1981 2010
Included observations: 30

Variable	Coefficient	Std. Error	t-Statistic	Prob.
C	1.100838	1.315746	0.836665	0.4110
GY	1.243306	0.218544	5.689028	0.0000
GX	0.051924	0.045630	1.137931	0.2664
R	-0.272030	0.149744	-1.816627	0.0818
D2	-4.451241	1.214349	-3.665535	0.0012
D4	6.600193	2.133042	3.094263	0.0050

R-squared	0.784618	Mean dependent var		6.786667
Adjusted R-squared	0.739747	S.D. dependent var		3.834214
S.E. of regression	1.956025	Akaike info criterion		4.356562
Sum squared resid	91.82479	Schwarz criterion		4.636802
Log likelihood	-59.34843	Hannan-Quinn criter.		4.446213
F-statistic	17.48599	Durbin-Watson stat		2.156324
Prob(F-statistic)	0.000000			

Simulations

GA

2010-11 = 0 to -5

2011-12 = 1 to 4

		(0,4)		
year	GA	GM	GS	GY
2010-11	0	4.911735	3.774469	3.303892
2011-12	4	7.371986	4.951307	5.366215
		(0,3)		
year	GA	GM	GS	GY
2010-11	0	4.911735	3.774469	3.303892
2011-12	3	6.787253	4.725631	4.89591
		(0,2)		
year	GA	GM	GS	GY
2010-11	0	4.911735	3.774469	3.303892
2011-12	2	6.20252	4.499954	4.425605
		(0,1)		
year	GA	GM	GS	GY
2010-11	0	4.911735	3.774469	3.303892
2011-12	1	5.617786	4.274278	3.9553

		(-1,4)		
year	GA	GM	GS	GY
2010-11	-1	4.327002	3.548793	2.833586
2011-12	4	7.234223	4.812465	5.255412

		(-1,3)		
year	GA	GM	GS	GY
2010-11	-1	4.327002	3.548793	2.833586
2011-12	3	6.64949	4.586789	4.785107

		(-1,2)		
year	GA	GM	GS	GY
2010-11	-1	4.327002	3.548793	2.833586
2011-12	2	6.064757	4.361113	4.314801

		(-1,1)		
year	GA	GM	GS	GY
2010-11	-1	4.327002	3.548793	2.833586
2011-12	1	5.480023	4.135436	3.844496

		(-2,4)		
year	GA	GM	GS	GY
2010-11	-2	3.742268	3.323116	2.363281
2011-12	4	7.096461	4.673624	5.144608

		(-2,3)		
year	GA	GM	GS	GY
2010-11	-2	3.742268	3.323116	2.363281
2011-12	3	6.511727	4.447947	4.674303

		(-2,2)		
year	GA	GM	GS	GY
2010-11	-2	3.742268	3.323116	2.363281
2011-12	2	5.926994	4.222271	4.203998

		(-2,1)		
year	GA	GM	GS	GY
2010-11	-2	3.742268	3.323116	2.363281
2011-12	1	5.342261	3.996595	3.733692

		(-3,4)		
year	GA	GM	GS	GY
2010-11	-3	3.157535	3.09744	1.892976
2011-12	4	6.958698	4.534782	5.033805

		(-3,3)		
year	GA	GM	GS	GY
2010-11	-3	3.157535	3.09744	1.892976
2011-12	3	6.373965	4.309106	4.563499

		(-3,2)		
year	GA	GM	GS	GY
2010-11	-3	3.157535	3.09744	1.892976
2011-12	2	5.789231	4.083429	4.093194

		(-3,1)		
year	GA	GM	GS	GY
2010-11	-3	3.157535	3.09744	1.892976
2011-12	1	5.204498	3.857753	3.622889

year	GA	(-4,4) GM	GS	GY
2010-11	-4	2.572802	2.871764	1.42267
2011-12	4	6.820935	4.39594	4.923001

year	GA	(-4,3) GM	GS	GY
2010-11	-4	2.572802	2.871764	1.42267
2011-12	3	6.236202	4.170264	4.452696

year	GA	(-4,2) GM	GS	GY
2010-11	-4	2.572802	2.871764	1.42267
2011-12	2	5.651468	3.944588	3.98239

year	GA	(-4,1) GM	GS	GY
2010-11	-4	2.572802	2.871764	1.42267
2011-12	1	5.066735	3.718911	3.512085

		(-5,4)		
year	GA	GM	GS	GY
2010-11	-5	1.988068	2.646087	0.952365
2011-12	4	6.683172	4.257099	4.812197

		(-5,3)		
year	GA	GM	GS	GY
2010-11	-5	1.988068	2.646087	0.952365
2011-12	3	6.098439	4.031422	4.341892

		(-5,2)		
year	GA	GM	GS	GY
2010-11	-5	1.988068	2.646087	0.952365
2011-12	2	5.513706	3.805746	3.871587

		(-5,1)		
year	GA	GM	GS	GY
2010-11	-5	1.988068	2.646087	0.952365
2011-12	1	4.928972	3.58007	3.401281

Simulations

GA: 2011= 0 to -5   2012= 4 to 1

GX: 2011= 8.2   2012= 6.8

GHR: 2011= 19.0   2012=20.9

	GA=(0,4)	GX=(8.2,6.8)	GHR=(19,20.9)	
	GA	GM	GS	GY
2010-11	0	4.814218	3.812867	3.300631
2011-12	4	7.469872	5.141079	5.495061
		GA=(0,3)		
	GA	GM	GS	GY
2010-11	0	4.814218	3.812867	3.300631
2011-12	3	6.870035	4.90018	5.012608
		GA=(0,2)		
	GA	GM	GS	GY
2010-11	0	4.814218	3.812867	3.300631
2011-12	2	6.285302	4.674504	4.542303
		GA=(0,1)		
	GA	GM	GS	GY
2010-11	0	4.814218	3.812867	3.300631
2011-12	1	5.700569	4.448828	4.071997

		GA=(-1,4)		
	GA	GM	GS	GY
2010-11	-1	4.229485	3.58719	2.830326
2011-12	4	7.317006	4.987015	5.37211

		GA=(-1,3)		
	GA	GM	GS	GY
2010-11	-1	4.229485	3.58719	2.830326
2011-12	3	6.732273	4.761339	4.901804

		GA=(-1,2)		
	GA	GM	GS	GY
2010-11	-1	4.229485	3.58719	2.830326
2011-12	2	6.147539	4.535662	4.431499

		GA=(-1,1)		
	GA	GM	GS	GY
2010-11	-1	4.229485	3.58719	2.830326
2011-12	1	5.562806	4.309986	3.961194

		GA=(-2,4)		
	GA	GM	GS	GY
2010-11	-2	3.644751	3.361514	2.360021
2011-12	4	7.179243	4.848173	5.261306
		GA=(-2,3)		
	GA	GM	GS	GY
2010-11	-2	3.644751	3.361514	2.360021
2011-12	3	6.59451	4.622497	4.791001
		GA=(-2,2)		
	GA	GM	GS	GY
2010-11	-2	3.644751	3.361514	2.360021
2011-12	2	6.009776	4.396821	4.320695
		GA=(-2,1)		
	GA	GM	GS	GY
2010-11	-2	3.644751	3.361514	2.360021
2011-12	1	5.425043	4.171144	3.85039

		GA=(-3,4)		
	GA	GM	GS	GY
2010-11	-3	3.060018	3.135838	1.889715
2011-12	4	7.04148	4.709332	5.150502
		GA=(-3,3)		
	GA	GM	GS	GY
2010-11	-3	3.060018	3.135838	1.889715
2011-12	3	6.456747	4.483655	4.680197
		GA=(-3,2)		
	GA	GM	GS	GY
2010-11	-3	3.060018	3.135838	1.889715
2011-12	2	5.872014	4.257979	4.209892
		GA=(-3,1)		
	GA	GM	GS	GY
2010-11	-3	3.060018	3.135838	1.889715
2011-12	1	5.28728	4.032302	3.739586

		GA=(-4,4)		
	GA	GM	GS	GY
2010-11	-4	2.475285	2.910161	1.41941
2011-12	4	6.903717	4.57049	5.039699
		GA=(-4,3)		
	GA	GM	GS	GY
2010-11	-4	2.475285	2.910161	1.41941
2011-12	3	6.318984	4.344814	4.569393
		GA=(-4,2)		
	GA	GM	GS	GY
2010-11	-4	2.475285	2.910161	1.41941
2011-12	2	5.734251	4.119137	4.099088
		GA=(-4,1)		
	GA	GM	GS	GY
2010-11	-4	2.475285	2.910161	1.41941
2011-12	1	5.149518	3.893461	3.628783

		GA=(-5,4)		
	GA	GM	GS	GY
2010-11	-5	1.890552	2.684485	0.949105
2011-12	4	6.765955	4.431648	4.928895

		GA=(-5,3)		
	GA	GM	GS	GY
2010-11	-5	1.890552	2.684485	0.949105
2011-12	3	6.181221	4.205972	4.45859

		GA=(-5,2)		
	GA	GM	GS	GY
2010-11	-5	1.890552	2.684485	0.949105
2011-12	2	5.596488	3.980295	3.988285

		GA=(-5,1)		
	GA	GM	GS	GY
2010-11	-5	1.890552	2.684485	0.949105
2011-12	1	5.011755	3.754619	3.517979

REFERENCES

Bergholt, D. and Lujala, P. (2010). Economic Effects of Natural Disasters and Armed Civil Conflict

Benson, C. and Clay, E.J. (2004). Understanding the Economic and Financial Impacts of Natural Disasters, World Bank

Christian R. and Jaramillo H (2009). Do Natural Disasters Have Long-term Effects on Growth?

Hallegate, S. and Ghil, M. (2008). Natural Disasters Impacting a Macro-economic Model with Endogenous Dynamics

Long, F. (1978). Impact of Natural Disasters on Third World Agriculture

Okuyama, Y. Economic impact of natural disasters: Development Issue and Empirical Analysis

Pelling, M., Ozerdem, A. and Barakat, S. (2002). The Macro-Economic Impact of Disasters.

Pelling, M., Özerdem, A. and Barakat, S. (2002).The Macro-economic Impact of Disasters. *Progress in Development Studies* 2, 4 pp. 283–305

Popp, A. (2006). The Effect of Natural Disasters on Long-run Growth.

Rasmussen, T.N. (2004). Macro-economic Implications of natural disasters in the Caribbean. IMF Working Paper

Rodríguez-Oreggia, E., Alejandro de la Fuente and Rodolfo de la Torre (2008).The Impact of Natural Disasters on Human Development and Poverty at the Municipal Level in Mexico. *United Nations Development Programme Regional Bureau for Latin America and the Caribbean*

Skidmore, M. (2007). Economic Development and the Impacts of Natural Disasters. *Economic Letters, Vol 94, Issue, pg 20-25.*
Toya, H. and Skidmore, M. (2005). Economic Development and the Impacts of Natural Disasters

Vatis, R. (2006). Complementing Natural Disasters Management: the Role of Social Protection

http://news.dawn.com/wps/wcm/connect/dawn-content-library/dawn/news/pakistan/provinces/06-us-will-help-flood-affected-balochistan-rs-02

http://www.reuters.com/article/idUSTRE66T3RS20100804

http://www.guardian.co.uk/global/blog/2010/aug/02/pakistan-floods-live-updates

http://www.bbc.co.uk/news/world-south-asia-10896849

http://floodrelief.punjab.gov.pk/RoadStatistics.aspx

http://urbanunit.gov.pk/DNAdata/01-%20Summary%20-%20updated%20Oct18-2010/01-%20summary%20flood%20damages%202010%20-%20oct%2018-2010.pdf

http://news.dawn.com/wps/wcm/connect/dawn-content-library/dawn/the-newspaper/business/slow-phutti-arrivals-mar-trading-on-cotton-market-210

http://news.dawn.com/wps/wcm/connect/dawn-content-library/dawn/the-newspaper/business/15pc-less-arrival-of-phutti-due-to-floods-600

http://www.sbp.org.pk/ecodata/Productselect.pdf

Made in the USA
Monee, IL
03 May 2026